NO LONGER PROPERTY OF
SEATTLE PUBLIC LIBRARY

P9-CKF-171

BACH
to the RESCUE!!!

How a Rich Dude Who Couldn't Sleep Inspired the Greatest Music Ever

by **TOM ANGLEBERGER**   illustrated by **ELIO**

Abrams Books for Young Readers • New York

Hey! It's me! Bach, the greatest composer ever!
Have I ever told you the story about Goldberg and the Rich Dude Who Couldn't Sleep?

Once upon a time, there was a Rich Dude who couldn't sleep.

Now, if a normal person can't sleep, they just have to deal with it. But this Rich Dude was so rich, he could pay someone else to deal with it.

So when this rich dude couldn't sleep—which was EVERY night—he would yell . . .

Goldberg was the Rich Dude's personal musician. I told you, this Rich Dude was RICH! He even had his own musician; and if he wanted to hear a song at 3 o'clock in the morning, then Goldberg was supposed to play it!

Unfortunately for EVERYONE, Goldberg lived in the basement. So, the Rich Dude had to yell "GOLDBERG!" really loud.

Even worse, Goldberg was hard to wake up, because he was still tired from being woken up the night before and the night before that and so on.

So, the Rich Dude had to yell REALLY LOUD.

And when the butler woke up, he would yell, too.

And when the maids woke up, they would yell, too.

GOLDBERG!!!!

Get out of bed, Goldberg!

Wake up already!!!

And when the rest of the village woke up, they would all yell, too.

FINALLY, Goldberg would sort of wake up, and the butler and the maids would push him up the stairs to the Rich Dude's room.

Now, if Goldberg played the flute or the harmonica or something, that would have been okay. But Goldberg played the harpsichord.

(A harpsichord is basically what they used for a piano before the piano was invented.)

Harpsichord, approx. 738 pounds

Now, the Rich Dude didn't want to get out of bed, so the maids had to carry the harpsichord up the stairs to his bedroom.

By the time they got the harpsichord up the stairs, Goldberg would have fallen asleep again. But the Rich Dude was still wide awake!

GOLDBERG!!!!! Wake up!

So finally, Goldberg was ready, the harpsichord was ready, the Rich Dude was ready, and the town was grouchy and grumbly.

But then . . . Goldberg would play.

He would play the most beautiful lullaby ever written.

And he would play it very beautifully, because he was a really good musician, after all.

And the villagers would stop grumbling, and they would say nice things about him as they drifted off to sleep one by one.

Soon the whole town was happily asleep.

Until . . .

So Goldberg would try a waltz . . .

and on and on and on until dawn.

The next day, the entire village would be tired and grumpy.

tired and grumpy dog

And the butler would be tired and grumpy.

And the maids would be tired and grumpy.

And the Rich Dude would be tired and grumpy.

And they ALL blamed Goldberg, who would have been tired and grumpy, except that he was asleep.

And then after a long day of being tired and grumpy, they would all go to bed tiredly and grumpily.

And just after they fell asleep . . .

GOLD BERG!!

and the whole thing would happen all over again!

I SHOWED UP!
(Don't I look nice? That's my best wig!)

Yep, it's me, Bach, the greatest composer of all time.

When it was time for me to go, Goldberg whispered in my ear . . .

Hmm, I don't know. Maybe.

Are you going to do it? Please! Pretty please! Are you? Huh? Please! You've got to help me! Please? Huh? Will you?

Listen, the Rich Dude is really picky, but he's also REALLY rich!

Hmm . . .

I didn't have time to compose anything right then, but being a wonderful person, I promised to help.

I can't wait to get out of here! Everybody's TOO tired and grumpy!

Bye-bye!

In the village, time passed slowly.

And everybody just got tireder and grumpier.

But I hadn't forgotten about Goldberg and his little problem. So, I took some leftover notes and a dance hall tune and an old folk song or something and mashed them all up, and it was the Greatest Music Ever Written Ever, and I stuffed it all in an envelope and sent it off. Yes, it's just that easy for me!

I'm Bach!

When they opened up my letter they found 32 little pieces of The Greatest Music Ever Written Ever. (Actually, it's only 31. I used one of them twice. Don't tell anybody.)

Goldberg locked himself in the music room all day to study the music.

And the butler liked it.

And Mabel and Blanche liked it.

And most importantly . . .

The Rich Dude liked it.

Ah . . . Goldberg . . . it's wonderful.

The next day, the happy and well-rested villagers had a parade and carried Goldberg and his harpsichord through the village in triumph!

(Goldberg slept through the whole thing.)

And that was how the Greatest Music Ever Written Ever was written by me. Or something like that.

The important thing is that everyone lived happily ever after!

Did they really? I have no idea.
All I know is that the Rich Dude sent
me a whole bunch of money!!!

Now THAT'S a happy ending!!!!!

Author's Note

This story is loosely based on Albert Schweitzer's account of Johann Sebastian Bach's creation of the *Goldberg Variations*. However, Schweitzer notes that it may not be true.

And while Bach may have been well paid for writing the *Goldberg Variations*, he seems to have written a lot of music for free or for fairly little payment.

But it doesn't really matter why Bach wrote the *Goldberg Variations*; I'm just glad he did.

My brain sometimes feels like I have a whole grumpy and tired village in my head. Everyone's yelling and shouting and complaining and carrying harpsichords around at once. It's not pleasant.

But listening to the *Goldberg Variations* seems to settle it all down. It restores order to my brain. Every note falls into the right spot. And it makes the village happy again.

Thanks to the internet, you don't have to be a Rich Dude to hear the *Goldberg Variations*. You can listen to and download an incredible performance by pianist Kimiko Ishizaka for FREE at opengoldbergvariations.org. (And if you want to try to PLAY like Goldberg, you can also download the sheet music there.)

To Sarah Reaser O'Brien,
the greatest piano
teacher ever!
—T.A.

To Genevieve.
Your laugh is music
to my ears.
—C.E.

The art for this book started as pencil on paper first.
Then digitally for darker lines and colors.

Library of Congress Cataloging-in-Publication Data

Names: Angleberger, Tom, author. | Eliopoulos, Chris, 1983- illustrator.
Title: Bach to the Rescue!!! / by Tom Angleberger; illustrated by Chris Eliopoulos.
Description: New York: Abrams Books for Young Readers, 2019.
Identifiers: LCCN 2018017973 (print) | LCCN 2018018524 (ebook) | ISBN 9781683354680 (ebook) | ISBN 9781419731648 (hardcover with jacket)
Subjects: LCSH: Bach, Johann Sebastian, 1685-1750.
Goldberg-Variationen—Juvenile literature. | Goldberg, Johann Gottlieb, 1727-1756—Juvenile literature. | LCGFT: Picture books.
Classification: LCC ML3930.B2 (ebook) | LCC ML3930.B2 A53 2018 (print) | DDC786.4/1825—dc23

Text copyright © 2019 Tom Angleberger
Illustrations copyright © 2019 Chris "Elio" Eliopolous
Book design by Pamela Notarantonio

Published in 2019 by Abrams Books for Young Readers, an imprint of ABRAMS. All rights reserved. No portion of this book may be reproduced, stored in a retrieval system, or transmitted in any form or by any means, mechanical, electronic, photocopying, recording, or otherwise, without written permission from the publisher.

Printed and bound in China
10 9 8 7 6 5 4 3 2 1

Abrams Books for Young Readers are available at special discounts when purchased in quantity for premiums and promotions as well as fundraising or educational use. Special editions can also be created to specification. For details, contact specialsales@abramsbooks.com or the address below.

Abrams® is a registered trademark of Harry N. Abrams, Inc.

ABRAMS The Art of Books
195 Broadway, New York, NY 10007
abramsbooks.com